Notebook

- This NOTEBOOK belongs to -

BRANDING BY Juls

www.ingramcontent.com/pod-product-compliance
Lightning Source LLC
Chambersburg PA
CBHW030939240526
45463CB00015B/410
9781691874293